W. C.

FROM PRAYERS TO PEACE

It All Begins with Faith

A Toolkit for Prayer

Phyllis Weaks Sanders, PhD

WESTBOW
PRESS®
A DIVISION OF THOMAS NELSON
& ZONDERVAN

Scripture quotations are from the ESV® Bible (The Holy Bible, English Standard Version®), copyright © 2001 by Crossway, a publishing ministry of Good News Publishers. Used by permission. All rights reserved.

WestBow Press books may be ordered through booksellers or by contacting:

WestBow Press
A Division of Thomas Nelson & Zondervan
1663 Liberty Drive
Bloomington, IN 47403
www.westbowpress.com
1 (866) 928-1240

ISBN: 978-1-9736-5662-3 (sc)
ISBN: 978-1-9736-5663-0 (hc)
ISBN: 978-1-9736-5661-6 (e)

Library of Congress Control Number: 2019902737

Printed in the United States of America.

WestBow Press rev. date: 8/22/2019

Dedications

I dedicate this book to my late parents, James and Doris Weaks, and my late grandmother, Alice Harris Weaks Plunkett, who taught me about the power of prayer, the need for faith in God's omnipotence (all-powerful), omniscience (all-knowing), and omnipresence (all around us), and the importance of remembering that Jesus Christ loves me (as my late Uncle Walter Weaks always told me).

I also dedicate this book to my fourteen-year-old cousin, Melanie Weeks, who wants to learn and understand more about God and prayer.

To my heart-to-heart sister friends and prayer partners, this book is supported by you, and it is also written for you as we continue our faithful and genuine friendship of laughing, crying, supporting and praying together for years to come.

To those favorite cousins who are also my friends, I dedicate this book to you for the multiple roles you play in my life and lifting me up in my heaviest times in life.

To my ninety-nine years old friend and mentor, Mrs.

Corine Cannon, thank you for your love, advice and enormous wisdom which allowed me to move forward and "let the rough side drag."

To My Amazing PAWS4Prayer Breaksfast Leadership Team and all Volunteers, this is your book!

To Jane Stewart Reid and Sarah Gillis Blackwell, my oldest family members, I praise God for you and your wisdom.

To my Sisters, Linda Weaks Southerland and Sharon Weaks Franklin, who share in the loss of our only brother, peace be with you and in you.

In Memory of my Brother, Dennis James Weaks

During the writing of the last chapter of my book, my brother completed his final chapter of life at age 63. I want to acknowledge my appreciation that our last conversation had to do with the need for prayer and ending our conversation with "I love you" and "I love you too". Our relationship was one of deep love and authenticity. We spoke openly to each other, agreeing and disagreeing but never engaging in manipulation or ulterior motives. We were charged with handling our parents' affairs together, and we handled them the same way—no manipulation or ulterior motives. We just wanted to help and give back out of love and gratitude for having amazing parents who did their best to teach us, support, guide us in decision-making and involve us in church and right living. While we weren't perfect by any means and did not always make wise choices, we did seek to move on to the next stage of life and learning, trying not to repeat the same mistakes. My favorite writing by my brother was in a note I found to a little girl when they were in the first grade. It read, "I love you said Dennis." I never let him forget that note, and I would say to him as an adult; "I love you said Phil." My love for my brother will always remain in my heart as I move From Prayers to Peace, peace that surpasses all understanding, and a peace that is draped in faith that I will see Dennis again one day.

Love,

Phil, Your Oldest Sister

In Memory of My Brother

Acknowledgments

I acknowledge with deep appreciation the blessing of family and friends who encouraged and supported the writing of this book.

My friend and prayer partner, Karen Williams, who gave her time and talent to read, offered feedback and wrote special prayers for special people in this work.

My friend and mentor, Elizabeth Bronson, for reading and proofing over and over again without complaint.

My friend of more than fifty years, Lauristeen Lovick, who read and shared her wisdom and inspiration.

My friend Mary Braswell, who traveled far to assist in the final production of this work.

My daughter, Phylisha Sanders, for her love and the writing of prayers for young adults.

My son, Maurice C. Sanders, Jr., for his art design in memory of his uncle Dennis.

I am thankful for Annette Davis for keeping me on task with her encouragement.

I am grateful to the WestBow Press Staff: Reggie Adams, Judy Luzon and Bob De Groffe. Also, a special thank you to Ashley Bullington who walked me through the final production stage with clarity and committed support.

I deeply appreciate the talent, skills and professional support from my nephew, Solomon Franklin, for understanding, conceptualizing and depicting the image I wanted on my cover design.

I am grateful to my five heart-to-heart Delta Sigma Theta Sorority sisters who are always on ready for helping me: Judy Murphy, Carmen Banks, Rev. Gail Nelson, Dr. Erica Fields and Melzina Cannon.

I thank the saints of Cedar Grove Presbyterian Church in Concord, NC for my spiritual preparation.

I am grateful for Joe and DeBrona Banks' continued, consistent encouragement and support.

I am most thankful to God for giving me health and strength to use my gifts to carry out the vision, mission, and ministry He has for my life. All to Him, I owe.

Testimonials

"This prayer book serves to teach the beginners, advance the intermediate, and promote the experienced in their daily prayers and understanding of how prayer matters". —Reverend Dr. J. Herbert Nelson who serves as stated Clerk of the General Assembly Presbyterian Church (USA), the largest Reformed Denomination in the United States.

"This book has strengthened my own prayers and taught me how to be more faithful and trusting during challenging times as I wait for God to respond His way." —Gayle Ricks, retired president and CEO of Growing Home Southeast.

"This book is just what is needed to do a study group on the power of prayer and the need to know how to pray in faith and live in peace, peace that surpasses all understanding." —Elder Elijah Washington, pastor of New Covenant Presbyterian Church.

"As a college student, I have learned from this book how to depend on God to meet all my needs." —Brooke Jones, student at North Carolina A&T State University.

"This book is a great gift of hope and faith in God and is strength for those who find themselves in dark places. The light that shines in this book enlightens the lives of people in need of prayer." —Rev. Dr. Alice Ridgill

"After reading this book on prayer, I know that, through prayer and faith in God, I am more than a conqueror through Christ Jesus." —Tiara Sanders, 2018 honor graduate of North Carolina Central University in Durham, North Carolina, who wrote "Prayer Thoughts for College Students."

"This book is a roadmap for understanding that prayer is the key to unlocking the doors of endless possibilities— personally and professionally."—Diann Monroe Jones, manager, third-party logistics, Xerox Corporation.

Preface: The Story
Phyllis Weaks Sanders

Prayer brings peace! After the doctor told me I had a tumor in my spinal cord, my first reaction was shock. I did not have any problems with pain in my back, just occasional pain in my right leg. In fact, I was jogging during that stage of my life. My second reaction listening to that news was fear, fear at the words, "An appointment has been made with the neurosurgeon." The word surgeon resounded the loudest. Then when I heard the prefix "neuro", fear and tears took over as the third reaction.

I did not stop to pray as an immediate reaction to the news of a tumor. I'm not sure that most people would do that initially. However, when I did stop later in the hour to reflect on the whole ordeal, I did pray. In the meantime, my close friends were already praying, trusting, and truly believing that everything would turn out for the good, for they said that God had a plan for me beyond this situation. Praying eased my mind from the rampant race it was running, and it replaced my fear with peace, peace that surpasses all understanding. My faith exploded.

I then kept my mind and spirit filled and fueled with scriptures, positive thoughts, and faithful outcomes of my surgery. Doing this proved great when I encountered the "gloomers" and the "doomers," those people who could only offer me the worst scenarios.

For instance, when people would tell me such things as, "Oh, my cousin had that surgery and he died," I responded, "I shall live." One lady said, "My uncle had that surgery and he was never able to walk again." I said, "I shall walk." I kept the positives in and the negatives out of my spirit. As a result, everything was successful, with no complications or major limitations even to this day, some seventeen years later.

I learned that all people can go from prayers to peace if they have the right tools for prayer. I started thinking about a prayer toolkit.

The main tool is faith. I appreciated the faith that my family and friends had and shared with me, but I needed my own faith, as well as a firm, steadfast faith that joined theirs and was not dependent on their faith alone.

The second tool is trust. I had to trust God regardless of the possible outcomes. I trusted God that my outcome would be total healing and restoration.

The third and most important tool is the Word of God—the Bible. To support my tools of faith and trust, I had to drape myself in healing scriptures. I Googled healing scriptures and found the ones referenced by Dodie Osteen, mother of televangelist, Joel Osteen. She not only read the healing scriptures; she wrote them down and read them every day and is still reading them even now that she is healed of cancer.

I actually experienced the value of writing scriptures down from a motherly spiritual mentor, the late Mrs. Johnnie Lee Nelson. She felt free to teach me and share with me some of her journals of faith and prayers because she referred to me as her daughter. She shared countless stories that I will save in a secret place in my heart. The lesson from this experience with her is to surround yourself with people of faith, and always have a person of wisdom who can lead you up Faith Street and Trust Avenue as you journey to healing, restoration, and any other challenges you may face. It is important to have motherly people in your life who pray for you on a regular bases and offer you Godly wisdom and advice. I have four other motherly women in my life, Elizabeth Bronson, Annie Hollis, Andrena Taylor and Hazel Waters. They spill out the truth about life and the power of God to help, to heal and to deal with life's unexpected introductions.

After recovering from surgery successfully and praising God for what only He did, I decided to venture out on faith again. During my six-weeks recovery period, I spent much time thanking and praising God and asking Him what He wanted me to learn from the experience. Did He simply want me to have quiet time to listen to Him? My thoughts ran rampant again. I decided that the first day that I was released to drive, I would go to the bank to inquire about how to buy a house, as I had forgotten what I did to buy my first house. After graduate school, I was tired of living in an apartment. I drove to what was First Union Bank at the time. Because I had spent the last three years in a doctoral program at the University of South Carolina with only a highly appreciated student assistant job in the office of the African American Professors' Program, my money was very limited. The surgery occurred before I had concluded a full year on my first professional job after graduation, so I was still playing catch-up with my bills after paying only minimum balances for three years. I was not ready to purchase a house; I simply wanted to know the steps to prepare for buying. There was no money in sight for a house.

After I answered some questions, the banker concluded the conversation by saying, "You might can get a $20,000 or $30,000 house."

I looked at him in dismay and simply said, "Thank you, sir." I chose to respond with the nature of the Fruit of the Spirit rather than the nature of the rotten fruit that he offered me.

I walked out of the bank and looked up to the skies and said these words: "My God is bigger than a bank and a banker. I will get me a house." That happened in 2001, and in 2004, the tool of trust was in full action as builders were laying the foundations of my new house, which was over ten times the projected goal that the banker gave me. He, I suppose, was operating on what he saw and heard. I was operating on what I did not see and hear. This incident began the second round of going from prayers to peace, knowing that it always begins with faith. After this experience of faith, every round of faith got higher and higher, and the tools in my toolkit for praying grew more numerous.

✦ My prayer toolkit began the day I heard about my tumor. The kit was laid with a strong foundation of faith. It was my faith that led to my prayers. The sidings of the toolkit were also draped with belief, and the top of the kit was covered with trust to keep doubt from entering to destroy my tools. The fragrance of the toolkit came from the Fruit of the Spirit and faithfulness.

After starting with faith, I moved from prayers to peace. Since that time, I have accumulated numerous tools that I use that take me from problems to prayers and from prayers to peace. The tools are called Scriptures, and it all begins with faith, faith in a mighty triune God: God the Father, God the Son and God the Holy Spirit.

Introduction

Prayer is simply communicating with God. We begin friendships and relationships by communicating with others. We share our good times with others, and as the relationship continues to develop, we begin to share our innermost concerns and challenges. The same can be true with prayer. If we start to share our daily thanks and appreciation for the good days and good times with God, before you know it, it becomes easier to share those times that grab us so unexpectedly and turn our smiles into frowns. Prayer is like a building block. Each time you block out time to pray, your blocks build peace and a comfortable relationship with Jesus and your desire to pray more gives credence to the Scripture of "Pray without ceasing," (1 Thessalonians 5:17). Before you know it, you will be speaking the words from an old spiritual song: "Now let us have a little talk with Jesus, and we'll tell him all about our troubles."

When you tell God about your troubles, you are doing just what He wants you to do—communicate with Him. Prayer is about glorifying, praising, worshiping, thanking, listening, and resting on His promise to receive a response from Him. He will hear your humble cry and will answer by and by; however, it will be in His way and in His time. The more you pray and communicate with Him, the more you will come to know and appreciate this about Him: His way is not your way. His time is not your time.

This book will give you the tools for creating your own personal prayer toolkit. I share my prayer tools with you, and you can add your own prayer tools as you move from prayers to peace.

Chapter 1
Essential Preparation for Praying

Part 1

Clear a place for meditation, quietness, and reflection. "Then Jesus went with them to a place called Gethsemane, and he said to his disciples, "Sit here, while I go over there and pray" (Matthew 26:36). Follow Jesus's lead. Go to a quiet place and pray.

Clean your heart of unforgiveness, malice, jealousy, hatred and sin as you set the stage for a renewed steadfast spirit for going to God in prayer. "Create in me a clean heart, O God, and renew a right spirit within me" (Psalm 51:10). A clean heart can contain an abundance of love.

Confess the areas of your life that you know are not pleasing to God. Your confession may or may not be a crime. Your confession could only be your negative thoughts, words, or behaviors. It could be a hot temper or stubbornness. If you want unlimited and unrestricted access for the Holy Spirit to have a full pass to enter your heart, humble yourself and confess your areas of weaknesses that need strengthening. "I confess my iniquity; I am sorry for my sin" (Psalm 38:18). Surrender and allow God to lead you down the path of righteousness for His name's sake.

Use the section below as a prayer guide to confess or write your weaknesses/sins.

Confess your weaknesses. Ask God for forgiveness, such as with the following: "Lord, I confess that I did not tell my friend the truth today. Forgive me, Lord."

I confess that...
Forgive me, Lord.

I confess that...
Forgive me, Lord.

I confess that...
Forgive me, Lord.

Part 2 Essential Preparation for Praying

Ask God to give you a daily intake of the Fruit of the Spirit. Galatians 5:22–23 tells us the Fruit of the Spirit are the following:

- **Love:** Practice your capacity to love everyone (1 John 3:18). It can be a challenge, but it can be done in God's love and strength.
- **Joy:** Search for joy in the midst of the storm (Nehemiah 8:10). It may be hard to find, but it is there somewhere, so don't give up your search.
- **Peace:** Seek peace when the storm is raging (Philippians 4:6–8). Holding firm to faith in God will give you peace that surpasses all understanding; just believe it and accept it.
- **Forbearance:** Wait with patience for God's timing (Hosea 12:6; Psalm 37:17). Let Him make the footprints for you to follow. Don't step ahead of Him, no matter how slow His pace may appear to be. It's time that matters the most—His time and not ours.
- **Kindness:** Express kindness in words and deeds (2 Timothy 2:24). Responding with kindness can tame an enraged tongue and shame inappropriate behavior. Avoid being unkind at all costs. Kindness brings double dividends in kingdom connections.

- **Goodness**: Model goodness in life's decisions (3 John 1:11). When goodness follows you, it creates blessings for others; stay in the blessing business for the rest of your life. It has an eternal profit.
- **Faithfulness**: Remain faithful in all situations (1 Corinthians 4:2). No matter what it looks like, sounds like, feels like, or smells like, have faith that God will see you through and get you through. He will never leave you.
- **Gentleness**: Show humility and gentleness to all (Titus 3:2). Replacing any type of haughtiness with humility and gentleness will gain self-control. Display self-control through godliness (2 Peter 1:5–7). Against such things there is no law (Galatians 5:23).

When you partake of the fruit of the Spirit, the carbs give you the energy and desire to follow God's commandment: "You shall love your neighbor as yourself" (Mark 12:31; Matthew 22:23; Leviticus 19:18).

Phyllis Weaks Sanders, PhD

The Fruit of the Spirit Prayer

Father, the One of power and dominion over my life, as I begin to pray, search my heart and cleanse it of all things that are not of You. Show me Your ways, dear God, and lead me down the path of righteousness for Your name sake. Allow me to remember the importance of a daily intake of the Fruit of the Spirit so that I can be filled with Your nutrients and nourishment for cleaner and better living. When others may attack me with insults, name-calling and other discouraging words, please give me strength and help me to model how the Fruit of the Spirit should look and respond. Cleanse my heart and clean my tongue of any foul words, idle words or language that don't glorify you. In Jesus's name, Amen.

Chapter 2
A Prayer Guide (and Only a Guide)

Many years ago, someone in her or his infinite wisdom created a model to help individuals learn how to pray. It is called the ACTS model of prayer. ACTS is an acronym used as a guide for praying. Each letter stands for a specific word that gives meaning and direction for praying. This model has helped numerous individuals who have attended the PAWS4PRAYER Breakfasts that I have conducted over 15 years and also in the Sweet Hour of Prayer study sessions that I conducted at my church. People in both prayer groups have successfully used this model as a foundation for developing a stronger, more confident prayer life.

Please do not allow arrogance and pride to tell you that you don't need a guide to learn to pray because you have been praying for years or you think all you need to do is talk to God as you would anyone else. God is not just anyone else. He is omnipotent, omnipresent, and omniscient. There is none like Him. Get beyond yourself and reach out to others who want to learn to pray with confidence and faith in the presence of others. People want to learn to pray aloud, anywhere and anytime. Some people need and want a step-by-step approach to learning. Take time to examine the ACTS model and use it for yourself or to help someone else, if you do not need it.

A   Adoration
C   Confession
T   Thanksgiving
S   Supplication

This mnemonic pattern of prayer is not a formula for praying or getting prayers answered. It is strictly a guide for learning some essential elements as you learn to pray openly or as you desire to strengthen your prayers. Let's begin.

Adoration: to worship and honor God's Holiness and His Sovereignty. To glorify and praise Him because He is the God of everything and everybody. He has reign over everything, and He is mighty in battle over all things. Kneel now before Him with deep adoration or lift your hands up to Him with praise.

Start your prayer with adoration, worship, or reverence to the Father, such as with the following prayer: "Heavenly Father, we recognize that You are the greatest Source and Resource we could ever have." Or this: "Eternal Father, I come before You today in the comfort of Your holiness and sovereignty in my life." Refer to Psalm 66:3 in your Bible for another example.

Think of some other ways you can give adoration to God, and then write them down.

_____

_____

Confession: to tell God about things you have done that you know are not pleasing to Him. (Of course, He already knows.) Confessing creates the pathway for seeking forgiveness for those sins you told God. Confession and His forgiveness create the pathway for cleansing the soul. Now you must believe that you are forgiven. When you truly believe you are cleansed, the comfort in praying has been established, and you are well on your way to learning to pray the way you desire because the blocks and barriers have been lifted.

Example: "Lord, I know that I am weak. I confess that I do not always have kind thoughts when others irritate me." Help me please.

Another example: "I know that my words are not always pleasing in Your sight. Forgive me, Lord." To understand more of how this works, refer to 1 John 1:9 in your Bible.

Write one confession for practice.

_____

Thanksgiving: to say thank you and to maintain a heart of thankfulness for all the great blessings you have already received. Having a grateful heart is thanksgiving. If you are reading this book, you are blessed, so thank Him for life, sight, insight, vision and provision.

Example: "Lord, I thank You for your grace and mercy. Thank you for allowing me to see the beauty of a new day and all other provisions you have made for me."

To help you understand this idea in more depth, refer to Psalm 69:30. Write one area of your life for which you are thankful.

_____

_____

Supplication: to tell God what you want or need for yourself or others. Keep in mind that God is all-powerful. When you pray, know that He is not too big to handle small things; nor is He too small for the things that are too big for you. God is omnipotent! Just ask Him! I promise that He can supply all of your needs. Ask!

Example: "Lord God, my family is in conflict right now and I need You to intervene and restore peace." Another example: "My close friend has just been diagnosed with diabetes. I ask that You supply all of his medical needs according to Your riches so that his body may be healed and restored." Turn to Philippians 4:6 in your Bible to know that it is okay to ask.

Practice writing a brief prayer request to God. Ask for something that you truly need. Think it; say it; write it and pray it.

_____

_____

You are almost there!

Currently, you have a B+, which means 90 percent of your learning how to pray is done.

To make it to an A+ using this prayer model, you have to pray this prayer and all prayers in the name of Jesus. Doing this alone makes this 10 percent of your learning greater than your 90 percent!

> "Ye have not chosen me, but I have chosen you, and ordained you, that ye should go and bring forth fruit, and that your fruit should remain: that whatsoever ye shall ask of the Father in my name, He may give it to you." (John 15:16)

Why pray in Jesus's name? Get your Bible and underline the following passages:

- Proverbs 22:1: "A good name is rather to be chosen than great riches, and loving favor rather than silver and gold." What better name is there than Jesus?
- John 14:13: "And whatsoever ye shall ask in my Name, that will I do, that the Father may be glorified in the Son." Be bold and courageous in praying in the name of Jesus.

Putting It All Together

As you read this sample prayer, put it in the context of ACTS Model.

Heavenly Father, I recognize that You are the greatest Source and Resource I could ever have. I know that my words are not always pleasing in Your sight, so I first want to ask for forgiveness for the way that I spoke to my coworker today. Lord, I want to thank you for allowing me to see the beauty of this new day and the opportunity for forgiveness and new mercies. Father, my heart is in pain for my friend, Carl. He needs You dear God. He has asked me to come and pray with him. Lord, my faith that You can heal is strong, but my confidence in praying out loud in the presence of others is weak. I pray that You will give me the confidence to step out in faith to pray in the presence of others, and I pray for the Holy Spirit to give me the right words to say. Hear my prayer in the Mighty Name of Jesus. Amen.

Where, When, and How Do I Begin to Pray?

I am so happy that you asked that question in your mind or spirit.

1. **Where?** Wherever you can find a quiet place without distraction.
2. **When?** When you have found your quiet and comfortable place of peace, it is time to gather your materials: your Bible, pen/pencil, and a journal (not a piece of paper).
3. **How?** Go to God in prayer with a clean heart, confidence in yourself, and faith in God that you can pray without the model and without fear. Read this Scripture before you pray: Psalm 27:1. "The LORD is my light and my salvation; Whom shall I fear? The LORD is the strength of my life; Of whom shall I be afraid?" Mark this Scripture in your Bible. Don't be afraid to learn to pray publicly when you can practice privately. God knows your heart, and He is pleased with your praying now. He wants you to grow in your prayer life, and He will strengthen you and give you the courage to bless others publicly through your prayers. Just watch and see!
4. Next, use ACTS to write out your next prayer. Choose one line from each sample and pray. For instance, choose only one from the three examples

provided in ACTS. You add real-life circumstances, conditions or petitions.

5. After you have prayed those selected lines at least three times, it is time to advance.

6. Next, get a journal or notebook and write your prayer using your own words as you follow the ACTS guide. Incorporate your own personal needs or desires. Use a real-life situation and people for whom you are praying. Make it real and relevant! God is waiting to answer your prayers. Start now.

7. For one week, write your prayers down and pray them out loud, making your wishes known to God. The more you do this, the more at ease you will become praying to the Father and blocking out all distractions, including fear of what others may think or say. You will replace fear with faith that God will continue to help you to pray and pray in the Spirit of the Lord. Praying is a beautiful way to communicate with God, the Father, through Jesus Christ. Maurice C. Sanders, Sr. in a telephone Bible study once said, "Prayer is talking to God through the voice and divine name of Jesus".

8. The next week, pray your prayers out loud without the model but with *your heart*. Make praying a priority and practice in your life.

It matters little what form of prayer we adopt ... or how many words we use. What matters is the faith which lays hold on knowing that He knows our needs before we even asks Him. That is what gives Christian prayer its boundless confidence and its joyous certainty.

—Dietrich Bonhofer, German theologian

Chapter 3
Faith: The Tool Needed for Answers to Prayers

Have you ever tried to drive or ride in a car without fuel? You may enjoy its beauty and comfort, but it won't get you where you are trying to go. So it is with faith. Faith, in relations to prayer, is the fuel you need to get your prayers going in the right direction to find the answers you need. God's will be done, not yours, remember? Read each Scripture below to help you to see the connection between faith and prayer.

Faith Scriptures

Use these Scriptures to help you to *pray and practice* faith. It must be done in the Spirit, because the flesh is too weak to grasp and sustain faith.

Matthew 17:20: He said to them, "Because of your little faith. For truly, I say to you, if you have faith like a grain of mustard seed, you will say to this mountain, 'Move from here to there,' and it will move, and *nothing will be impossible for you."*

Matthew 21:21: "And Jesus answered them, 'Truly, I say to you, if you have faith *and do not doubt*, you will not only do what has been done to the fig tree, but even if you say to this mountain, 'Be taken up and thrown into the sea,' it will happen.

Mark 10:52: And Jesus said to him, "Go your way; *your faith has made you well."* And immediately he recovered his sight and followed Him on the way."

Hebrews 11:1: "Now faith is the assurance of things hoped for, *the conviction of things not seen."*

1 Peter 1:21: "Who through Him are believers in God, who raised Him from the dead and gave Him glory, so *that your faith and hope are in God?"*

Just in case you missed the point about faith, let me say it this way:

> *Faith in prayer is a must, not an option.*
> *Faith in prayer is a need, not a want.*
> *Faith in prayer is an answer, not a question.*

Make Faith and Prayers Partners in Communicating with God

Just as believing comes before seeing, faith comes before prayer. Prayer and faith must be communication partners as you seek to have your spiritual and personal development plans fulfilled. Prayer is communication with God, and prayer can communicate your thoughts and thanksgivings, your desires, even your frustrations and disappointments to God. Man and woman were created to fellowship with God. Praying is a valuable opportunity for getting all that we need in this life through this fellowship; however, an attitude of faith must accompany prayer.

Faith is a word that is often used so loosely. People will sometimes say to others in distress what sounds like a slang or trite phrase: "Keep the faith." Others who proclaim to be followers of Christ might say, "I prayed, but nothing happened so I stopped praying." Still, there are those who say, "You got to have faith, but God gives you common sense." None of these bland statements reflects the strong faith needed for praying. Once you establish your faith, then your prayers can lead you to peace. Determine your level of faith. Consider the different types of faith that a person can have at one time or another.

Mustard seed faith is the tiniest faith one can have and hold while it grows into the largest and greatest answer to your prayer. The mustard seed is referenced in the Bible in the parable and used as a metaphor for the Kingdom of heaven: "The Kingdom of heaven is like a mustard seed planted in a field." It is the smallest seed (in biblical times), but it became the largest of garden plants that grew into a tree where birds could rest and find shelter in its branches (Matthew 13:31–32).

Mustard seed faith combined with prayer can do the

same in your life. Something exceedingly small, like a mustard seed, will grow to be exceedingly large, like a mustard seed plant, if you allow your faith to accompany your prayer. Can you cite an example when you had mustard seed faith that grew into strong branches of support for you and others? Read and write out Matthew 13:31–32 in your prayer journal.

Flip-flop faith is a combination of trust and doubt. You trust one minute; you doubt the next. Flip-flop faith is usually based on seeing and feeling. The old adage of "Seeing is believing" is not always true. Seeing should not always mean believing. We do not always see the whole of any view at first glance. Sometimes we only see a part of it and try to make it a whole. When this occurs, it can cause us to flip in our faith and believe in our sight. The same is true for feelings. Feelings are governed by circumstances; even the change of the weather can affect your feelings. When the sun is shining, we feel good. When the clouds are dark and it is rainy, we feel blue. Faith cannot be based on what you see or what you feel. It must be stable and steadfast. If you are controlled by what you see and the feeling that derives from the sight, you may flip in your faith and flop in your prayer. John 20:29 says, "Blessed are they that have not seen and yet have believed." Repeat this verse three times, then write it from memory in your prayer journal.

Folding faith is giving up when things do not turn out your way. Have you ever prayed for something and you received the opposite, such as healing for a friend or a loved one? Was there ever a time when you asked God for help in dealing with a belligerent child and the child became worse? After you did not get what you asked for, did you feel like folding up and giving up on God? Most of us have experienced folding faith. Reflect on a time when your faith folded. What lesson did you learn from the experience? Did the message come directly from God or through someone He sent to you? God did not promise life without storms, but He did promise to help you weather the storm. Weathering any difficulties requires faith. Everything has an end and faith helps you to reach the end. God demonstrated His faithfulness to us when He sacrificed His only begotten Son so that we may have a life in Christ. Write one suggestion you can give to someone who is experiencing an episode of folding faith. Write it in your prayer journal for relevant use.

Firm, steadfast faith is solid as a rock, believing with no seeing and no wavering, no giving up and no doubting, just standing and waiting on the Lord. Firm, steadfast faith is knowing that God is going to keep His promises and respond to your prayer requests in due time. His response may not be what you asked for, but you can rest assure that it will be in your best interest and for the best situation for your circumstances. Remember, God sees the big picture, the past, the present, and the future. Our sight is very limited, and that is why it is important to have firm, steadfast faith in God to direct your path and accept His will for our lives.

In your prayer journal, list three ways you will try to incorporate firm, steadfast faith in a current challenge you are facing.

Faith can be defined in Hebrews 11:1; verse 2 tells how faith helps us understand the world; and verse 3 tells who received a good report for having faith. Examples of faith can be read in verses 4–39 (Hebrews 11:1–39. After you answer the questions below, read chapter 11 of Hebrews.

Consider these questions for self-reflection.

1. Do you consider yourself a faithful person?
2. In what ways do you encourage others to be faithful?
3. Considering the four kinds of faith described (mustard seed, flip-flop, folding or firm, steadfast faith), which do you model the most? Which one of these types of faith do you want to be your faith legacy for your children, spouse, brothers, sisters, relatives, and friends?

From Faith to Prayers to Practice

By now, I hope you have realized the importance of faith and prayer working together as partners to get answers to your prayers. Faith requires practice; practice requires action.

In 1 Peter 1:21, we are told that faith and hope should

be in God. If your faith and hope are in God, then you are ready to use a real-life and relevant prayer need for God to intervene and bring solutions for you. Write your prayer using the ACTS guide in Chapter 2.

A.

C.

T.

S.

Add these lines to your prayer: "Lord, this prayer request is too hard for me to handle, so I place it in Your hands. I remain faithful to Your work, Your will, Your way, and Your Word. No matter how You answer my prayer, I will continue to trust and obey You. I will be still and know that you are *God*."

Chapter 4
Everyday Prayers for Everyday People in Everyday Lives

Prayers in this chapter are written by the following:

- Karen Brown Williams
- Phylisha Y. Sanders
- Tiara Nicole Bell Sanders

When You Want to Pray and Can't

You pray for me, and I pray for you. Prayer opens up the heavens for all types of blessings to fall. Yet there are times when your heart is too heavy to pray. Use these prayers to get you through difficult times. The only direction for praying these prayers is to pray with faith, knowing that God is listening and desires to respond. Pray with the assurance that He will answer according to His Will, and pray without ceasing for Him to live in you with Jesus as your Source of Strength. Use the Scriptures as your resources for deepening your faith and the Holy Spirit as your voice for your guidance. Have listening ears as you trust and obey, for there is no other way but to have firm, steadfast faith with these prayers. The journey from prayers to peace begins with faith.

A Prayer of Thanksgiving

Father,

I thank You for everything. Lord, You have searched me and have known me. I am naked but not ashamed before You. You know me. You know my frame. You know my past. You know all there is to know about me, and You still love me. I thank You for the forgiveness of my sins. Your Son, Jesus, died a cruel, harsh death for me. Greater Love hath no man! I thank You! You hear my cries. Create in me a clean heart and renew a right spirit within me. You see me as I am. You are not moved by my faults, failures, mess-ups, bad attitudes, willfulness, and arrogance. You are moved when I come to you just as I am without one plea, but that Jesus's blood was shed for me. Nothing else matters. As I abide under the shadow of the Almighty, keep me there. Give me strength to resist the deceptions of this world: the lust of the flesh, the lust of the eye, and the pride of life. I am nothing without You. Your very breath fills my lungs. My life depends on You. God, I thank You! Hear my prayer in Jesus's name. Amen.

A Prayer for People Who Are Sick

Sovereign Lord,

You created me. Your Word tells me that I am fearfully and wonderfully made! Praise the Lord! You know every inch of my physical body. Father, because sin is in this world, I have problems. Sickness comes. I know You as the Great Physician. I know You as a Healer. Father, when sickness racks my body, it scares me. Disease makes my body weak and vulnerable. I feel helpless. Lord, I need your help when I am sick and the sickness appears to be unto death. I have no one to call on but You. Father, as I recall the healing of the lepers and the lady with the issue of blood and the little girl and later Lazarus raised from the dead; when I recall the blind man who had his sight restored and the man whose withered hand was restored and the many other instances where Jesus healed, I know there is hope for me. My hope is in God. Hear my earnest plea for healing. Jesus bore my sins in His body on the tree; therefore, I am dead to sin and alive unto God, and by His stripes I am healed and made whole. Heal me, Lord. I will live and not die and declare the works of the Lord! I will prosper and be in good health!

In the precious name of Jesus, I pray.
Amen.

A Prayer for People Experiencing Financial Difficulties

Father,

Thank You for Your provision over the years. Lord, even though finances become tight and sometimes there is no money for anything, You always make a way. I know that You do not intend for me to live in constant stress because of finances. Father, help me keep a heavenly perspective. Money is a means of exchange. Your Word tells me that I should be content with a place to live, clothes to wear, and food to eat. Teach me to be grateful for these things. This world attempts to make me feel that I can't live without more than that. I want to please You. I am so very grateful to You for what you have provided for me. Help me to be obedient to your Word and wise with Your provision. You know the monthly bills are due and the car needs gas and maintenance, the children need clothes and shoes, and unexpected situations come up, but they were not unexpected to You. Protect my finances from the evil one. Help me to follow Your Word for my finances, to always honor You with the first tenth of all of my increase, to give offerings, to be wise and to be generous. Your Word tells me that good measure, pressed down and shaken together and running over, will be poured out for me. Your Word tells me that You shall provide all of my needs according to Your riches in glory by Christ Jesus. Plant Your Word deep down into my soul and spirit. Lord, I want whatever you have for me. I want to be content. Like Paul, I want to know how to live on little and to live with plenty. Whatever the circumstances may be, when I count my blessings and name them one by one, You have provided for me exceedingly and abundantly beyond all I can ask or think. Thank You! I love You!

In Jesus's name, Amen.

A Call for Immediate Help

Lord, Please help me. Help me right now, Lord. I need you! Cover and protect me. Amen.

Lord, I need your attention right now; I do not know what to do. Speak to me; show me, Lord. You are my shepherd! Amen.

Lord, Lord! Jesus, Jesus, what shall I do? Speak to me, Lord Jesus. Amen.

Prayer for Families Dealing with Conflict

Father God,

The family is ordained by You. When You are the center of the family, even though strife, disputes and disagreements may arise, Your love covers. Peace returns and families thrive. Thank You for my family. Help me to be a peacemaker in my home. Heal hurts. Your Word teaches us that love is patient and kind; it does not envy or boast; it is not proud, rude, self-seeking, or easily angered. It keeps no record of wrongs, does not delight in evil but rejoices with the truth. Love always protects, trusts, hopes, and perseveres. Love never fails. God, You are Love.

We sometimes forget these things in my family. We want to be right. We want to have the last word, no matter how harsh that word may be. Lord, help us to esteem each other more than ourselves. Help us to be forgiving and to remember that You forgave us for all of our sins against You. Bring peace to our home. We invite You in, Father. Clean up our home and make it a place where You want to dwell. Bring us close together. Bind us into an unbreakable cord. I speak peace over my family.

In the matchless name of Jesus, Amen!

Phyllis Weaks Sanders, PhD

A Prayer for People with Arthritis

Lord,

I need the touch of Your healing hands to soothe my aches. This pain is constant and unbearable sometimes, and I bring it to You in the name of Jesus. Almighty God, please give me relief in my bones and joints. Ease my pain when I walk, when I sleep, and as I go through the day, trusting in You and leaning on You. Anoint me with the power of the Holy Spirit and break the yoke of this pain. Restore me to wholeness. Breathe the breath of healing upon me. Lay your healing hands upon the areas where I hurt the most. Give me the strength to pray even when I am in pain so I can lift up my eyes unto the hills from whence cometh my help, because my help is in You. Because You are Jehovah, Rapha, the one who heals, I pray this prayer in Jesus's name. Amen.

A Prayer for Caregivers

Father,

I praise Your Holy Name! Thank You for the love You give me. Thank You for peace. Thank You for mercy. Lord, I need Your help. There is no other help I know. I thank You for my family member whom I love so much. Oh, how she has blessed my life. But, Father, right now she needs me more than ever. She requires daily care because she is now unable to care for herself. Father, please give me the strength I need to take care of her in a way that glorifies You and gives her rest and peace. I count it a privilege to be able to do this. But I do get tired juggling her care and keeping up with my other responsibilities. Lord, You are my Great Supply, so now I ask that You supply me with strength to care for my loved one and myself. Your Word says You give power to the faint, and to them who have no might, You increase strength. Lord, increase my strength. Help me to speak words of comfort and love to her. Please help me never to make her think that she is a burden. Help me to convey how much of a blessing she is to me and how much You love her. Thank You for all You do for us.

In the powerful name of Jesus, I pray. Amen.

Phyllis Weaks Sanders, PhD

A Prayer for the Person Who Needs and Receives Care

Gracious God,

The One who gave His only Son that we may live and be forgiven, I call on You today to speak to my heart, cleanse it, and make me acceptable unto You. You know my conditions. My pain is hard to bear sometimes. Lord, in my worst pain and agony, keep my words soft and my spirit humble before You and all those You have sent to be my caregivers. Let the words of my mouth and the meditation of my heart be acceptable in Thy sight, and show appreciation to my caregivers. When I can do for myself, let me not put unnecessary burdens on my caregivers. When I can assist with my own care, give me that extra dose of strength to help myself. Let me be reminded that in the midst of my circumstances, I am still wonderfully blessed. Lord, please help me keep basic words flowing from my mouth: "Please"; "Thank you"; "I appreciate what you are doing for me;" "I thank God for you and all of His blessing." Father, keep Your Word and Scriptures of salvation, healing, wholeness, and restoration resting in my heart, reminding me of whose I am.

I offer this prayer in the matchless name of Jesus Christ. Amen.

A Prayer for Me and My Illness

My God, through Jesus Christ, I come to You with deep humility but boldness in my faith that You can help me. You know my need even before I pray it because You are all knowing, but Your Word tells me to pray. I know that I do not always pray as I should because sometimes, Lord, I feel like my condition is just my lot in life. Then I am reminded of Your word, which tells me that the thief comes only to steal and kill and destroy and You came that I may have life and have it abundantly. Lord, the thief has come trying to kill me with a disease/condition called _____. Though I am on medication to help me, Lord, I pray that you will heal me so that the medication will not be needed. I know that You are the Healer, and I have seen Your healing power throughout the Bible and in my family and friends. Now I am praying that You will remove the thief and its deposits in my body that are trying to destroy and kill. Please reach down and touch my weak body with Your healing touch and restore it with Your breath of new life for me and my body. Please supply my doctors all their needs, according to Your healing riches. Father, I stretch my hands to Thee; no other help I know. I praise You and thank You for hearing and answering my prayer.

Amen.

A Prayer for Wayward Children

Lord,

I love You! You are the only One with the power I need to handle the issues surrounding my child. I thank you for my child. My child has chosen to live a life outside Your Will and outside of what he/she has been taught, having been raised in the nurture and admonition of the Lord. I prayed when he/she was in my womb with an expectancy that this child would bring joy to our family. I prayed for his/her body to be healthy, for him/her to be strong in Spirit and to live a prosperous life. I prayed that he/she would accept Your free gift of forgiveness and salvation through Christ and know for himself/herself the great love You lavishly pour out on him/her. I prayed that my child would choose You, have a relationship with You, and live a life committed to You.

Lord that is not what I see. Conversations are difficult. There is disrespect and unacceptable behavior in my home, a home where You reside with us. Father, my child was trained in the way he/she should go, so I know when he/she is old, he/she will not depart from it. But right now, Lord, it's hard for me. I pray, and I cry sometimes, but I recognize the enemy is trying to kill, steal, and destroy my child. But in Jesus's name, I declare Your truth that all things work together for the good of those who love God and are called according to Your purposes. The devil is a defeated foe! Lord, You have taken care of every scheme of the devil. Father, I'm preparing for battle! I go into battle to take what the enemy has tried to steal from me—my child. I'm a mother, and that's what we do! In Jesus's name, my loins are girded with truth. My feet are shod with the preparation of the Gospel of peace. I have put on my helmet of salvation and breastplate of righteousness. I have the shield of faith in one hand and the sword of the Word of God in my other hand. Father, You are my protection in this battle. I plead the blood of Jesus. I thank You that I am the victor and so is my child. When this battle is over, I pray that my child will know the great lengths You took to save him/her. Because of Your grace and mercy, there is nothing that he/she has done that love will not cover and forgive. Love keeps no record of wrongs. Father, pour Your strength and wisdom into me and take my hand. Lead me, direct me and guide me. My eyes are fixed on You. This battle is not mine. It's Yours! Bring my child back.

In Jesus's mighty name, Amen.

Phyllis Weaks Sanders, PhD

A Prayer for Our Leaders

Sovereign God,

You are our Leader. It was under Your leadership that the world was created. By Your power, You created man and woman. Thank You, Almighty God, because had it not been for you, the person who wrote this prayer and the person who is reading this prayer would not exist. We stand in awe of Your creative leadership. You are so awesome! We worship You in spirit and in truth. Thank You for providing for our needs and many of our wants. Thank You for jobs, money, homes, automobiles, clothes on our backs, shoes on our feet, and churches and places where we worship. Most of all, thank You for Your grace and mercy, spiritual products that can only come from You.

We approach Your throne to ask You, our Highest Commander in leadership, to provide divine wisdom to our national leaders whether they ask for it or not. They need You, Lord, and we must intervene on their behalf as they make daily decisions that can impact the world You created. You have blessed our nation with prosperity. You have given us freedom that people in other countries don't have. Please guard the hearts of our leaders so that their hearts may beat to the rhythm of principles and promises of Jesus. We pray for a praying leader, one who seeks You first. Please prevent our leaders from being self-serving.

Serving You first will keep our country moving from prayers to peace. In the Name of the One Who Makes Constant Intercession Before the Throne on our behalf, Jesus, the Christ, Amen.

Phyllis Weaks Sanders, PhD

A Prayer for Educators

Heavenly Father,

We exalt You, and we magnify Your name. We confess that we do not always call on You as we should, and there is really no excuse, but our hearts are sometimes so heavy that it weighs us down in disgust and depression before we can even go down on our knees in prayer. Teaching has changed. It is very difficult and challenging. The honor of teaching has been minimized by test scores. Not only are children not passing these tests devised by humans, children are not passing Your tests because the basic ten commands and prayer are no longer allowed in the institution of learning. Forgive us, Lord, for allowing one atheist woman and other individuals to push lawmakers to expel God's Word from our schools. Now, Dear Father, we are bombarded with problems that have affected the ability and freedom to teach and learn in peace. We are faced with safety issues: children fighting teachers and staff; teachers molesting children; parents coming to school buildings cursing educators and students; domestic deputes intruding the learning process by threatening harm to teachers, children, and staff; people coming in our schools to kill and destroy the joy of teaching and learning; and a multitude of other issues that need Your attention. Thank You, God, for giving us a heart and mind. We can pray without ceasing, without technology and digital cameras recording our prayers from our hearts. Please cover all educators with your protective shield, which blocks out satanic attacks from those who are missing the opportunity to learn about You. For the success that we are able to make in the midst of these challenges, we thank and praise You. For the strength that You pour in our spirit that keeps our spiritual engines strong, thank You. Now God, we ask that You help us to balance school life with family life and church life. In each of these important institutions, we need Your presence. We pray this prayer in the name of the Master Teacher, Jesus Christ. Amen.

A Prayer Message to College Students

As college students, we may stray from God and our daily acts of holiness due to having more freedom and living off the edge of life. A great essential for college is to learn to pray, or if you are comfortable praying, to engage in prayer morning and at night. Prayers can actually be prayed any time, orally or silently.

One prayer that you might want to consider praying sounds like this:

Dear God, I would like to thank You for blessing me with an amazing family and genuine friends who support my journey through college.

I know that I will be faced with trials and tribulations while in college. I know that You will take care of me and I can depend on You to help me through any struggles. I have a desire to pray to You every day, in good times and bad. Keep me strong that I may not be distracted from my studies and from my home training. Send me people who know You, Lord Jesus. I pray that You will keep me close so that my relationship with You will grow closer each day that I am in college and thereafter. I write and pray this prayer in the name of Jesus, my Savior. Amen.

When Unexpected Conflict Enters the Family

Father God, I thank You that you are my Mighty Counselor and I can come to You in good times and challenging times. I am thankful that You receive all the praises that I send up to You in all times. I thank you that you also receive my stresses, my disappointments, my heartaches, and my headaches. Today, Lord, I come for directions, directions on what to do with a family member whom I have given temporary shelter in times of her/his storm. Days and months have passed, and I don't see much evidence of my relative making progress to move toward independent living again. Yet, there is no physical or mental reason that restricts him/her from working and saving money to move. Lord, I want to ask her/him to prepare to move in the next two months, but I feel guilty. I am also reminded of the scripture that says, "But if anyone does not provide for his relatives, and especially for members of his household, he has denied the faith and is worse than an unbeliever." Lord, I am not an unbeliever, and I am not denying my faith. I just want my peace restored. I am asking You to speak to me, show me, and teach me what to do and how to get my peaceful home back. Show my family member what to do. Open his/her eyes to see possibilities of independent and faithful living. Open up windows of opportunities for her/

him to find peace and restoration from his/her troubled times and bad decisions. Father God, hear my prayers and grant me an answer to my dilemma. I leave this prayer in the hands of Jesus, Your Son and my Savior, Amen.

A Prayer of Thanks

Thank You, Father, for the blessings You have continuously bestowed upon me. You are *so* good. You make me smile. Yesterday was a good day, but today is going to be a better and more awesome day. Tomorrow is going to be an even better day than today. Thank You for Your faithfulness to me. Thank You for giving me strength during the difficult times. I thank you for the plans that you have for my life. Thank You for showing me Your design for family. Show me how I can reach out and be an example of family in someone else's life. Thank You for accepting and embracing me always. I thank you for making me a better person. I am growing every day. I thank you for listening to me. I thank you for your revelations. I thank you for being in my life. I thank you for protecting me. I thank you for loving me, even the few times when I am not being lovable. Bless me abundantly! Bless my family, friends, coworkers, the sick, the shut-ins, _____, _____, _____, and _____. Bring healing to their bodies. Lord, I pray for_____. Give him/her peace. Please continue to enlarge my territory; place favor over my life. I am grateful for Your plans for yesterday, today, and tomorrow. Thank you God that new doors are opening and favors and blessings are coming my way. Thank You for being in control. Thank You that these valleys are leading me to higher and better levels in my spiritual life. All in the name of Jesus, I pray. Amen.

Phyllis Weaks Sanders, PhD

A Prayer for Relationships

Father God, whose graciousness never ceases,

Thank You for taking me to new places seen and unseen. Thank You for supplying all my needs according to Your riches in glory. Heavenly Father, today I choose to honor You by honoring the people You have placed in my life. Thank you for bringing genuine and positive people into my life and helping me not to have to directly deal with the negative. Please protect me from the negative people in my life and allow the Holy Spirit to fall afresh on them. Lord, make me more effective on my job. Please increase the quality of my relationships by helping me to model Your way and not mine. I want more people to love and encourage. I submit my resources to You today and ask You to show me where I can sow seeds and be a blessing to those around me. Show me how to love others the way You love me so that faith will grow stronger in my heart. Enlarge my territory so that I can be a greater blessing to those around me. Open doors that no man can close, and pour out Your abundance in every area of my life! I believe that with You, all things are possible! Make Your truth about _____ real to me today. Please comfort and heal_____.

In the name of Jesus, Amen.

A Prayer of Faith

Heavenly Father,

Today, I repent for anything that I've been confessing that isn't pleasing to You. Show me if there is anything in my life that is displeasing to You so that I can walk with You all of my days. Father God, I choose today to keep my mind and heart focused on Your Word. Lord, I know that the Bible says that faith without works is dead. I have faith and want my words and actions to reflect it. Today, I will take a step of faith and declare my trust in You. Even though I might not see how, I know and declare that You are working behind the scenes in my life. I have faith, and as I act on my mustard seed faith, allow me to see it grow stronger and stronger so that I will live in victory every day! Father in heaven, today I open my heart to You and all that You have for me. I ask You to bless me. Help me to understand Your truth so that I can make Godly choices. Help me to broaden my perspective so I can fully live and experience the full life You have for me. Lord, I ask You to teach me to be faithful to You always. Thank You for depositing seeds of faith in my heart so that I can live in total victory. Show me where to give or sow seeds that I have so that I can reap the harvest You have prepared for me. Heavenly Father, thank You for bringing increase in every area of my life. Thank You for choosing to live inside me. Show me the treasures You have deposited within me

Phyllis Weaks Sanders, PhD

so that I can fulfill Your purpose for me all the days of my life. Fill me with Your faith, peace, joy, and love so that I can overflow with Your goodness today and every day. I want to have firm, steadfast faith in You.

In Jesus's name, Amen.

A Prayer of Trust

Heavenly Father,

I humbly come to You today. Thank You for Your blessings and benefits in my life. I choose to focus on Your goodness and believe You have so much more in store for me. I honor You today in all I do. Father God, thank You for the good plan You have for my life. I choose Your plan and ask that You direct my mind and thoughts according to Your purposes. Heavenly Father, I want everything You have in store for me. Today, I choose to align myself with You. Today, I choose to trust and rely on You. I know You are a Faithful Deliverer. I cast all my disappointments, anxieties, worries, troubles, concerns, fears, and cares on You, because I know You care and want the best for me. Thank You for saving me! I love You and need You.

In the name of my Savior, Jesus, Amen.

A Prayer for Young Adult Ladies and My Future Husband

Father God,

You are omniscient, and I thank you for the plans that You have for my life. Thank You for showing me Your design for family. Show me how I can reach out and be an example of family in someone else's life. Thank You for accepting and embracing me always. I thank you for the men that You have sent me. Though the relationships did not last, I thank You for Your spirit of discernment that has shown me who was real and those that were not right for me. I have grown having known them all. Help me not accept the bottom when I have You at the top. Help me to respond in peace when someone tells me the clock is ticking, or you better have a baby soon. Give me the continued strength to wait on You and Your time. Thank You for the man that is going to be my husband. I don't know who he is, but I have faith that he is going to be everything that I want and need. Make him real to me and me real to him. Order our steps so that we grow spiritually, personally, professionally, romantically, and financially as individuals, as friends, as a couple, as husband and wife, as lovers, as parents, as a family, as Christians, and as partners. Prepare us now so that when the time comes, we will be ready. Bless us now and when we come together. Let us have firm, steadfast faith as You bring us together. Armor us so that no weapons formed against us prospers. Strengthen us and bless us now during the difficult times and during the good times. I pray that he is able to lead our family and our relationship according to your Word. I pray that he will speak words of faith, that he prays for us and knows and believes that You are taking care of us and promoting us.

In Jesus's name, Amen.

Prayer about My Not-So-Good Day

Father God,

Your grace and mercy are given to me every day. Thank You that everything that I am doing and going through is preparing me for my future. Thank You for what You are doing and for what You are creating just for me. I know that what I am going through is going to help me to do all that You need and want me to do for You and your kingdom. I am releasing every negative thing that has happened to me today. I am releasing every hurt, worry, and disappointment. Lord, I know that disappointments are inevitable but misery is optional. I choose to trust You and Your plan. I choose to not be angry, bitter, and depressed. I choose to believe that You are opening doors, making divine connections, and strengthening me. Thank You!

I am forgiving the people who did me wrong. The sun will not go down on my anger. Lord, I am going to bed in peace.

In the wonderful name of Jesus, Amen!

A Prayer for Women in Prison

Father in Heaven,

You are so merciful. In spite of what I have done, I am surrounded by Your power and goodness. I come to You asking for Your forgiveness for this crime I have committed. When I made the decision to break the law, I was thinking only of myself. Though there is no good reason to commit a crime, I thought that somehow it would make things better for me, and I never thought I'd end up in prison. But I am here, and I realize the huge mistake I made. I regret it. Your Word says, "If we confess our sins, You are faithful and just to forgive us of our sins and cleanse us from all unrighteousness." Please forgive me. I ask that you help me to do better in my life. I am sorry for what I did to those victims of my crimes. I am sorry that I am putting my family through this difficulty. I am especially sorry for what this is doing to my children. They are all suffering because of my bad choice.

Lord, I know that when I come to you in humility and I pray to you with a sincere heart that you hear me. Please keep me safe in this dangerous and lonely place. You are my Protection. Make me a light to shine in the darkness of prison. Your Word says that You came to set the captives free. I know that I will be physically behind bars for a while, but my mind can be free from anger, hostility, self-pity, wrong thinking, and negativity. I can still open my

Phyllis Weaks Sanders, PhD

mouth to sing and shout praises to You, and as Your Word says, "Bring my soul out of prison that I may praise Your Name."

I pray that You will keep my children safe, protected, and covered with Your strong love. They need me, and I'm not there for them. I place them in Your hands. Keep them encouraged. Guide them in their daily lives and their decisions. Provide for all of their needs according to Your riches in glory through Christ Jesus. Surround them with people who will show them love and kindness. Give them the peace that surpasses understanding. Take care of them please.

For those whom I victimized, Lord, I ask Your forgiveness. Please repair the damage I caused. I pray that Your peace will be upon them. And I pray that one day they will forgive me.

And Lord, in the Bible, as You were with Joseph, John, Paul, and Silas when they were in prison, please be with me. Give me wisdom from above. I pray for restoration. I pray that You will give me rest at night when I go to sleep. Bless me with a renewed and transformed mind focused on You and Your Love, Mercy, Kindness, and Goodness toward me. Your Word says with God nothing shall be impossible, so Father, I pray that You push the reset button in my life and give me another opportunity to live my life for good and to Your Glory, whether here in prison or out of prison. I thank You that Your Son, Jesus, has redeemed me from all my sins, and I am forgiven because He died a prisoner's death on the cross for me. Thank You, Lord!

I put all of my trust in You. Thank You for hearing me. In the mighty and supreme name of Jesus I pray, Amen.

Phyllis Weaks Sanders, PhD

The Prayer of Salvation for Women in Prison

Heavenly Father,

Your Word says that *everyone* who calls upon the Name of The Lord *shall* be saved. I want to be saved, so I am calling out to You with my whole heart and asking You to forgive me for my sins even though I am behind these bars. I accept Your forgiveness. I believe that Jesus died on the cross for me. I believe that He died, was buried, and rose again. I believe that He is now sitting on the right hand of God, the Father, praying for me. I believe that He has made me brand new, that old things have passed away and all things are new. I believe that Jesus loves me just as I am without one plea but that His blood was shed for me. I believe there is no condemnation for me because I am in Christ. And I believe that I will be in heaven with Him the very minute He calls me home. I am forgiven! I am the righteousness of God in Christ Jesus! Thank You, God! I want to live the rest of my life trying to please You more than I please myself. When I do, it becomes a new freedom for me, and no longer am I in bondage. Thank You, God. Thank the Lord I'm free.

In my Savior, Jesus's name I pray.
Amen.

Prayers for Our United States Servicemen and Women

Our Lord, our God,

You are my Commander-In-Chief. You laid out Your orders in the Holy Bible. You are such an awesome and on-time God. I trust You with my life and my family's life. I honor Your Holy name, the name above all names.

I am a soldier in the military, serving my country as best I can. I pray that you will strengthen me for this honorable service to my country. While I am away from my family, cover them with Your shield of protection. Increase their faith in You to know that You will take care of me and they do not have to worry. Help them to believe and know that I am not just a soldier in the military. More importantly, I am a soldier in the army of the Lord, and as a result, I trust that no weapons formed against me will prosper. I praise you for our country and the opportunity to serve. In Christ I pray, Amen.

Our Lord, our God,

I know family members and friends who are enlisted in the military. The world is volatile, and I know anything can happen at any time. Your supreme power controls the world because, after all, You do hold the world in Your hand. I pray, Dear Father, that as the world turns, more and more people will know that You are still in charge, regardless of how things may appear. When we become fearful about our family and friends in the military, remind us of the words in Psalms that say, "Be still and know that I am God." I ask for Your divine protection for all the men and women who serve our country. I pray that they will draw closer to You each day. I thank You for the gifts of grace and mercy in their lives. Let the anointing of the Holy Spirit fall afresh on every soldier each day of their service. Bring them safely back home to their families and friends. In Jesus's name, Amen.

Precious Lord,

Take the hands of all soldiers in our military and lead them safely through any battle that they may face. First, give them the armor of God and keep their faith and trust connected to You. Then, Dear Lord, let no weapons formed against me prosper—no, not one.

In the name of Christ, I pray. Amen.

Prayer of Salvation for Someone

Almighty and Powerful God,

I come to you today, interceding on behalf of _____

_____. As one who believes in You, Your Son,
Jesus Christ, and the Holy Spirit as one Triune God, I
know that it is Your desire for all people to be saved and
come into the family of believers and worshippers of Jesus
Christ, so I bring _____
before you right now. Whatever _____is
doing that is not of Christ, I pray that You will break the
bondage of evil, ill intent, sin, and oppression from him/
her in the name of Jesus. Wherever he/she may go, I pray
that there will be someone there to share the good news
of Jesus Christ. Open _____'s heart to feel
the spirit, open his/her ears to hear the words of the good
news, and open his/her eyes to see the glory of an Almighty
and Powerful God who saves. Lord, let him/her feel Your
presence, experience Your grace and mercy, and recognize
that these gifts cannot be bribed, bought, or borrowed.
These gifts come from You and You only. Teach him/her to
know and understand that Jesus died and was resurrected
for all of us, we can be forgiven for our sins, and we can
be saved. Help him/her to believe and have faith because
salvation is acquired by faith (as stated in Ephesians 2:8)
and receiving Jesus as his/her Lord and Savior (as found in

John 1:12). I pray that he/she will find a Scripture, a person, a Bible, a story, or an experience to bring him/her to the light of Christ. Please save _____ in Jesus's name I pray. Amen.

Prayer for Law Enforcement

Father, as our city police officers, county sheriff officers, highway patrols and all security officers who have shields of protection for the people, please place your strong arm of protection around each officer each day. Lord, guide their hearts and heads that they may make wise decisions in dealing with people of all races, ethnicities and those with challenging behaviors. We pray that the Holy Spirit will lead them as their assigned angels surround them. Continue to breathe the breath of life upon them and bless their families. Please keep them in perfect peace with their eyes stayed focused on You. In Jesus's name. Amen

Chapter 5
A Spiritual Body Workout: Exercising for Greater Use

One Body and Many Members: Many Members with Different Uses

1 Corinthians 12:12: "For just as the body is one and has many members, and all the members of the body, though many, are one body, so it is with Christ."

Romans 7: 21-23: "So I find it to be a law that when I want to do right, evil lies close at hand. For I delight in the law of God, in my inner being, but I see in my members another law waging war against the law of my mind and making me captive to the law of sin that dwells in my members."

Isaiah 33:15-16: "He who walks righteously and speaks uprightly, who despises the gain of oppressions, who shakes his hands, lest they hold a bribe, who stops his ears from hearing of bloodshed and shuts his eyes from looking on evil, he will dwell on the heights; his place of defense will be the fortresses of rocks; his bread will be given him; his water will be sure."

Ephesians 4:15-16: "Rather, speaking the truth in love, we are to grow up in every way into him who is the head, into Christ, from whom the whole body, joined and held together by every joint with which it is equipped, when each part is working properly, makes the body grow so that it builds itself up in love."

Exercising for the Eternal Fitness Center

Our body was not created for physical purposes only, even though some people go through their entire life using their body for only physical purposes. God designed us to nurture our physical body with physical and spiritual food and to use our physical body as a temple for spiritual purposes and our spiritual body to keep our physical body aligned with God's expectations for our temple. God wondrously made us, and we should constantly be aware of both our physical health and spiritual health. To remind us of the essential use of our body for spiritual growth and physical development, let us focus on members of our human physical body for spiritual use.

The Spiritual Use of Your Hands

- Use your hands to help, not to harm.
- Use your hands to lift others up, not to push them down.
- Use your hands to knead the bread of life and give it to those who are hungry and need to be spiritually fed.
- Use your hands to reach out to your community and invite them to join you in your feast on the Word of God.
- Use your hands to extend the right hand of fellowship with one another, no matter what the person looks like, smells like, or talks like.
- Use your hands to cover your mouth when unkind words are trying to push through.
- Use your hands to help shape and mold the lives of children for knowing and serving Jesus Christ.
- Use your hands to catch friends, family, and church members who may be falling by the wayside of life.
- Use your hands to lead someone to Christ.
- Use your hands to lift up praise and honor to Almighty God, the One who is omnipotent, omniscient, omnipresent and the One who gave you helping hands.

Lord, the hands that You gave us came from Your Creation, and they cannot be duplicated or replicated to their original state in which You made them. Let us be thankful for our hands and use them as the hands of Jesus to help others as You would have us do. We pray that we will use our hands to continue to carry out the ministry of Jesus Christ as we seek to know and serve Him better through helping others with our gifted hand. If anyone is without physical hands, help them to discover other ways to share the Good News and good deeds with others. Thank you for all other ways they can serve communities and nations. In Christ we pray. Amen!

The Spiritual Use of Your Feet

- Use your feet to stand up. Stand up for Jesus.
- Use your feet to help you carry the heavy crosses that may have come so unexpectedly in your life. Then let your feet lead you to the foot of the cross, where you can lay down your burdens and leave them.
- Use your feet to take you to the place where Jesus has called you to be for such a time as this. Bask in your spiritual gifts and glorify Him in your work.
- Use your feet to step to the beat of God's purpose for your unique life.
- Use your feet to kick habits of fuming with anger over things you cannot control. Use your feet to stamp out igniting fires that distract you from praising and honoring God in all circumstances.
- Use your feet to run from the worship of people, objects and places as idols and use them to run miles and miles to Jesus and for Jesus.
- Use your feet to leave footprints that will lead more people to Christ.
- Use your feet to climb the rungs of God's ladder to reach your ultimate height—heaven and everlasting life.
- Use your feet to go and teach communities, neighbors, neighborhoods and nations the Gospel of Jesus Christ as He commanded.

Our Father and our God, thank you for your infinite wisdom and sending us a Savior. You sent your Son, Jesus, to take away our footprints as He uses His feet to carry us and deliver our burdens to You. Help us to rely more and more on Jesus as we struggle with issues with family, aging, other dilemmas, marriages, and, yes, even our faith. There are times when we have not completely gone through one trial before we are faced with one or two more. Each trial carries its own set of fragile moments where we just want to run and hide from everyone, to simply seek refuge for our souls. We pray that during these fragile moments of our lives, You will allow the breath of the Holy Spirit to fall afresh on us, delivering prayer power and peace power through Jesus Christ, our Savior and Your Son. Amen.

Phyllis Weaks Sanders, PhD

The Spiritual Use of Your Eyes

- Use your eyes to read the Bible for life's instructions.
- Use your eyes to see the beauty of a new day of life.
- Use your eyes to watch the rising of the sun and the going down of the same.
- Use your eyes to see the needs of children and help them to see your goodness through the eyes of Jesus and His love for them.
- Use your eyes to see what God created for free but what now comes with a price: the ocean, air, water, trees, dirt, etc.
- Use your eyes to see visions of growth and increase in your own holiness for living a righteous life.
- Use your eyes to see the impossible through the Designer's spiritual lenses called faith.
- Use your eyes to read and learn that you can do all things through Christ who strengthens you.
- Use your eyes to close and visualize God answering your prayers.
- Use your eyes to see when others need encouragement: a card, a hug, a smile, or a "checking on you" call.
- Use your eyes to see the beauty of family, friends, and fun.
- Use your eyes to see how you need to rest, relax, and rejoice in the Lord!

Lord, how mighty is Your Name in all the earth. I rest my eyes on You as I look unto the hills from which cometh my help. I thank you for physical sight, spiritual sight, and divine insight that comes from You. Grant me good health so that I may stand strong to do your work and will in my life, as I use my eyes to gaze at the beauty of your creations. I pray in Jesus's name. Amen.

The Spiritual Use of the Tongue—
Exercise with Care

- Use your tongue for speaking the language of love and the forgiveness of your debts and your debtors as you prepare for the kingdom of heaven.
- Use the tip of your tongue to remind you that words may temporarily hurt your feelings or make you angry, but keep your tongue wagging with words that strengthen your soul and make others feel whole, not broken but whole.
- Use your tongue to lick out bitterness from the crevices of your heart because bitterness is an attack on *your* heart, not on the other person.
- Use your tongue to pray, praise, and spread the Gospel of Jesus Christ.
- Use your tongue to pray for your church, asking God to lift any strains and stresses that indicate unbelief about the power of God to supply all of your needs according to His riches in Christ Jesus.
- Use your tongue to give thanks for members of your family who know and believe in Jesus as their Lord and Savior, and then let all who believe use their tongues to pray for others to join the family of Christ.
- Use your tongue to answer God when He calls you out of darkness into the marvelous light.

- Use your tongue to give praise to God when things in your life are at their worst or at their best, because God is the same awesome God in both situations.

- Use your tongue to taste the goodness of life so that when distasteful words are spoken to you or about you, you are not left with a bitter taste and bitter heart. Rather, have a prayerful heart for the person who spoke the bitter words. People's words reveal their hearts. When they have a bitter heart, use your tongue to pray for them.

- Use your tongue to taste and see that the Lord is good; blessed is the one who takes refuge in Him.

- Use your tongue to speak encouraging words, words of wisdom, not foolishness and meaningless words with no substance.

- Use your tongue to practice telling people, "I love you and God does too."

Our Father, Your name is to be raised and praised. Lord, tame my tongue; keep it from being too loose. I confess that at times I am weak and weary and my tongue speaks words that are not words of faith and wisdom. Sometimes I am a victim of someone else's tongue that spurts out words of doom and gloom. Yet, I know that you are the Light of the World and Your light brings clarity and peace to any situation when we put our faith in You. Help me not to always see or speak the negative. Don't let my negative past experiences reflect in how I respond to others. Allow me to speak truth and strength that came from my past so that I can measure the goodness of the grace that got me through my past and into the light of God. Please remind me to use my tongue to praise and not complain; to speak life and not death and to speak joy in Jesus's name. Amen.

Spiritual Use of Your Nose

- Use your nose to smell the fragrance of the Holy Spirit sweetly moving to speak to you and rescue you from harm's way.
- Use your nose to sniff the smell of righteousness when others are creating odors of injustice.
- Use your nose to breathe fresh air when the air of pollution seems to encircle your surroundings.
- Use your nose to sniff out cold airs of destructive comments that others may drift your way.
- Use your nose to inhale the power of God, the love of Jesus, and the sweet Holy Spirit as they work as one Triune God to keep you loved, covered and safe.
- Use your nose to exhale any contaminated or toxic breezes that angry winds may pass your way.
- Use your nose to detect and blow out the smell of deceit, malice, jealousy and destructive thoughts.
- Use your nose to smell the sweet fragrance of God, the One who gave you your nose as a significant body part of His mighty creation so that you can breathe the breath of life with praise and thanksgiving to Him.

Almighty God, Creator of Heaven and Earth, Your power to create in us a body that has a purpose that is absolutely divine. Lord, we are so thankful for Your omnipotence (power) and omniscience (all knowing) that brought all of our body parts into one body, each with its own purpose to make up one body for the purpose of serving You and working to recruit other bodies for the kingdom. I pray that I will be a recruiter for You. I pray that You will use my nose to give me a keen sense of smell for Your children who need help, who are searching for truth, who are struggling with the issues of life and those who need a word from the Lord. Help me and show me how to use my nose to inhale the full joy of serving you through Jesus Christ our Lord. Amen.

Spiritual Use of Your Toes

- Use your toes to help you walk down the path of holiness.
- Use your toes to wiggle with joy and peals of laughter.
- Use your toes to constantly reach for your higher calling in life.
- Use your toes to balance your life steps and not to sway too far from Jesus.
- Use your toes as you help others to balance and support their walk with the Lord.
- Use your toes to tiptoe quietly in your special place for meditation and prayer.

Father, it is in Jesus's name that I pray this prayer for the use of members of my body that I sometimes take for granted or give little attention. I pray that you will bless my toes that I may always have a balanced life as I stand on my tiptoes to reach for my spiritual assignments from You each day. Shine Your light on me and allow the spirit of the living God to fall afresh on me. I ask that You melt me, mold me, fill me, and use me. Amen and Amen!

Spiritual Use of Your Ears

- Use your ears to listen when God is trying to tell you something.
- Use your ears to hear the voice of Jesus calling in the night.
- Use your ears to hear the sweet sound of the Holy Spirit guiding you in the right direction.
- Use your ears to listen to the chirping of the birds to remind you that if God will take care of the birds, He will surely take care of you.
- Use your ears to hear the music and songs that lift up the name of Jesus in praise and honor.
- Use your ears to listen to the voice of the Holy Spirit bringing you a message for your next call and assignment from the Lord.
- Use your ears to listen to the silence of peace.
- Use your ears to hear people who are calling out for help, love and attention.

Omnipotent, Omniscient, and Omnipresent God, let us always be attentive of the Triune God who speaks to us in more than one way with more than one purpose. We thank You that you gave us ears to listen. Let us listen attentively to the voice of the Holy Spirit to direct our path in life. In Christ I pray. Amen.

Spiritual Use of Your Knees

- Use your knees to bend down to pray.
- Use your knees to bend down to talk to a child about Jesus.
- Use your knees to bend down to plant a garden of hope, peace, and love to another person.
- Use your knees to bend the pride out of your life.
- Use your knees in humility before the throne of God to seek forgiveness for any hurt or harm you may have caused in your life or in the life of someone else.

Gracious God, We bend and bow to You with a thankful heart for the power that You have in the world and in our lives—the power to heal, to comfort, and to bring about change that we know is impossible for us. Thank you for knee power in Jesus's name. Amen.

Phyllis Weaks Sanders, PhD

Know the Spiritual Symptoms of a Heart Attack

- When your heart for others is shallow.
- When your heart bleeds disdaining, hurtful words upon other people.
- When your heart pumps more worldly wisdom than Godly wisdom into the lives of other people.
- When your heart does not beat with the rhythm of Jesus.
- When your heart no longer filters in any portions of understanding of the blood of Jesus and you can't say, "I love you."
- When your heart and the hardening of the arteries block the Holy Spirit.
- When your heart resists and blocks a time for devotions, scriptures and prayer.
- When your heart becomes empty of the fluid of forgiveness.
- When your heart is revived by people you think have positional power and not by God's promises and power.
- When your heart pumps blood of hatred and evilness.
- When your heart is clogged with unforgiveness and stubbornness.
- When the rhythm of your heart beats faster than the rhythm of God's timing.

Heavenly Father, please bless our hearts. In the name of Jesus. Amen.

How to Keep a Healthy Spiritual Brain

- Never think more of yourself than you do of God and His children.
- Exercise your brain in the spiritual gym we call church and worship.
- Maximize your thoughts and actions in spiritual matters that can make the world a better place to live when you use the brain that God gave you.
- Keep your brains exercising for the Lord; it prevents stiffness and damage to the soul.
- Keep your vessels clear of debris of sin, doubt, unforgiveness, and hatred so that the love of God can flow freely from you to others.
- Take daily doses of the Word to prevent toxins from leaking into your brain and affecting your mind.
- Supplement your brain with Vitamin D to understand God's *divine* purposes for your life.
- Supplement your brain with Vitamin C to stay *Christ-centered.*
- Supplement your brain with Vitamin K to *keep* the memory of His grace and mercy in your life.
- Supplement your brain with Vitamin B-12 to *be* like the 12 disciples, remembering their legacy and experiences with Christ.

Phyllis Weaks Sanders, PhD

- Supplement your brain with Vitamin A to *always* keep God first in your life.

Lord, strengthen my brain so that I can think of Your mighty works and Your power in me to do all things through Christ, who strengthens me. Keep me clothed in my right mind. From your power, please maximize my power to think before I speak, praise before I complain, and pray before I speak words that are not fitting for Your purpose and plan. Keep me focused and disciplined. I pray that you keep my brain healthy that I might have a Christ-like mind. I pray this prayer in the marvelous name of Jesus Christ, our Lord. Amen.

… And we know that for those who love God all things work together for good, for those who are called according to his purpose. A spiritual body workout is essential in keeping fit for the kingdom of God. Have faith in God and confidence in yourself by saying, "I can do all things through him who strengthens me." Your spiritual body workout helps to take you from prayers to peace when you warm up with faith in the Triune God, the One who created you and sustains you. Before praying, think about faith in these ways.

Faith before prayer is a must, not an option.
Faith before prayer is an answer, not a question.
Faith before prayer is a need, not a want.

Chapter 6
Praying in Faith, Living in Peace

Praying is an act of communing with a mighty God. As stated in Chapter 2, prayer was defined as talking to God through the voice and divine name of Jesus. Many people pray, but the important message in this definition of prayer is the importance of praying in the name of Jesus. Faith must be present in praying in the name of Jesus. When one has faith in praying through Jesus Christ, there is substance in prayer, and that substance is called faith. Hebrews 1:1 describes faith as substance. It also describes faith as evidence. Have you ever prayed about something that you really needed or wanted but you could not see any visible signs of it coming? Yet you trusted anyway and had faith that God would make it happen? That is called evidence of things not seen. Praying in faith removes anxieties and worries when you cannot see, hear, or even feel any evidence but your faith remains and allows you to live in peace any way. In the book of Judges, when Gideon built an altar, it was called, "The Lord is Peace." When you pray in faith, your peace is in the Lord. Your prayers can transcend to peace when you allow faith to have its beginning place prior to going into prayer.

Phyllis Weaks Sanders, PhD

Reflections and Recordings

How has my prayer life changed as a result of reading this book?

_____

_____

_____

What was a "wow" moment for me?

_____

_____

_____

Name three people you think could benefit from reading *From Prayers to Peace*.

1. _____

2. _____

3. _____

How will you ensure that they will receive this book and read it?

_____

_____

What will you do to keep your faith active and strong?

_____

_____

Do you think your prayer life will change? How?

_____

_____

Are you more comfortable praying after reading this book?

_____

_____

Are you ready to pray in public, beginning with faith in your prayers and confidence in yourself?

Yes____ No____ Explain.

How will you design your prayer toolkit? There is always a need to pray. What will you put in your prayer toolkit to keep you committed to praying without ceasing?

Start a small prayer group to study this book. Use your feet to step in as a prayer group leader and see God bless you in a mighty way, OR use your tongue to ask someone else to lead and see how God will bless both of you and all of you.

I believe you are ready for a new prayer life, and that through Jesus Christ, you will have a strong, discipline prayer life. *You* can do all things through Christ, who strengthens *you* as you go from Prayers to Peace; it All Begins with Faith and A Prayer Toolkit.

CONGRATULATIONS!

Certificate of Prayer Power

_____ has used this book to learn more about prayer, peace, and faith on the _____DAY OF _____, 20_____, and will practice reading and praying this verse that will be an essential tool for a Prayer Toolkit.

"Do not be anxious about anything, but in everything by prayer and supplication with thanksgiving let your requests be made known to God. And the peace of God, which surpasses all understanding, will guard your hearts and your minds in Christ Jesus."

As found in Philippians 4:6–7 and believed by Phyllis Weaks Sanders, PhD